Wild Animal Kingdom

GRAY WOLVES

GAIL TERP

BLACK
RABBIT
BOOKS

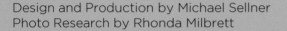

Bolt is published by Black Rabbit Books
P.O. Box 3263, Mankato, Minnesota, 56002.
www.blackrabbitbooks.com
Copyright © 2017 Black Rabbit Books

Design and Production by Michael Sellner
Photo Research by Rhonda Milbrett

Library of Congress Control Number: 2015954918

HC ISBN: 978-1-68072-051-8   PB ISBN: 978-1-68072-308-3

Printed in the United States at CG Book Printers,
North Mankato, Minnesota, 56003. 8/17

Web addresses included in this book were working and appropriate
at the time of publication. The publisher is not responsible for
broken or changed links.

Image Credits
Adobe Stock: hkuchera, 12 (bot-
tom); Alamy: blickwinkel, 11; Corbis: nge-
la to Roxel/imageBROKER, 26–27; Dreamstime:
Designpicssub, 18; Iakov Filimonov, 6–7; Getty:
Daniel J Cox, 8 (top); Wilfried Martin, 4–5; iStock:
KeithSzafranski, Cover; Dennis Donohue, 17 (top); jim-
kruger, 21; karlumbriaco, 16–17; Kenneth Canning, 22–23;
Marc_Latremouille, Back Cover, 1; NEALITPMCCLIMON, 24;
weisen007, 23 (bottom); Shutterstock: abrakadabra, 14, 19
(silhouette); Andrew Astbury, 31; ArtHeart, 14; Derek R. Au-
dette, 12 (top); Ilya Andriyanov, 23 (top); JAMES PIERCE, 29
(deer); jo Crebbin, 32; Mageon, 29 (plant); pandapaw, 8–9;
Rudmer Zwerver, 29 (mouse); Tom Tietz, 3; Ultrashock,
29 (wolf); Valentyna Chukhlyebova, 29 (moose)
Every effort has been made to contact copyright
holders for material reproduced in this book.
Any omissions will be rectified in subse-
quent printings if notice is given
to the publisher.

Contents

CHAPTER 1

A Day in the Life

A **pack** of six gray wolves searches the woods. One wolf picks up the smell of deer. Time to hunt. It's a cold day, but the wolves' thick fur keeps them warm.

The wolves follow the deer scent to the edge of their home **range**. They stop to howl. Their howls warn other packs they are there.

100
80 **120**
60 **140**
40 **160**
20 **180**
0 **200**
pounds pounds

WEIGHT
40 TO 160 POUNDS
(18 TO 73 KILOGRAMS)

SHOULDER HEIGHT
27 TO 36 INCHES
(69 to 91 centimeters)

Supper Time

The wolves spot three deer. One looks sick. It walks slowly and falls behind. The wolves draw near. When close, they rush at the deer. Two deer run away, but the sick one falls. Time to eat.

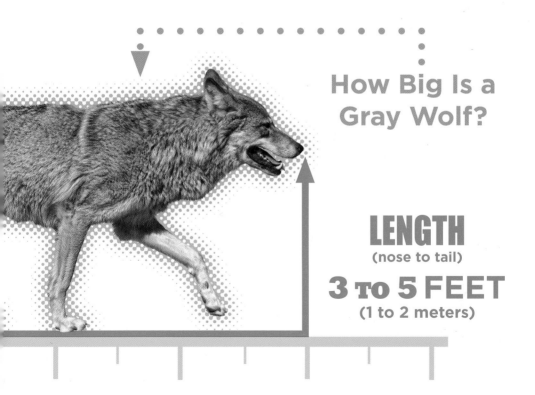

How Big Is a Gray Wolf?

LENGTH
(nose to tail)
3 TO 5 FEET
(1 to 2 meters)

THICK FUR

LONG TAIL

EARS

BLACK NOSE PAD

LONG LEGS

CHAPTER 2

Food to Eat
and a Place to Live

Gray wolves are **carnivores**. They hunt large **prey**, such as moose. They also hunt small prey, such as mice. A wolf might not eat for days. But then it can eat up to 20 pounds (9 kg) of food at one time.

Home Sweet Home

Gray wolves live in many places. Some live in forests. Some live in grasslands or **tundras**. Their home range can be more than 1,000 square miles (2,590 square kilometers).

Wherever they live, most gray wolves hunt in packs. They seek out young, old, and sick prey. Healthy prey is too hard to catch.

Hunting in Snow

Snow with a hard crust can help wolves hunt. Their wide paws help them run on the crust. But large prey gets stuck in the snow.

WHERE GRAY WOLVES LIVE

Gray Wolf Range Map

CHAPTER 3

Family Life

Most gray wolves live in packs of four to nine wolves. Each pack is led by a male and female. These two leaders are the ones that have pups. They also lead most hunts.

Colors

Not all gray wolves are gray. Some are white and some are black. One pack can have gray, white, and black wolves.

GROWING
FAST

Pups

Gray wolf pups are born in dens in the spring. A den could be a rock cave. It could also be a hole in the ground. Most **litters** have five to six pups. The pups stay in the den for about six weeks.

Before the pups learn to hunt, the pack feeds them. First, the wolves hunt and eat their catch. Then they throw up the meat for the pups to eat.

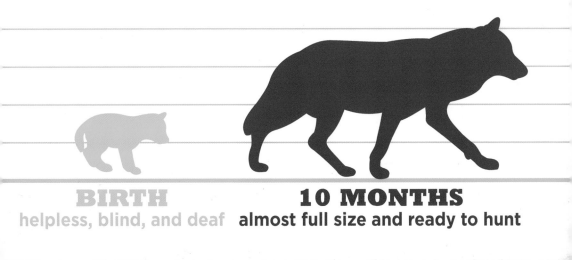

BIRTH
helpless, blind, and deaf

10 MONTHS
almost full size and ready to hunt

A New Home

Mother wolves move pups from den to den throughout the summer. The pups learn to play and run. All pack members help care for them. The pups watch what the adults do. Then they practice on their own. They learn to be good pack members.

By the Numbers

175 POUNDS (79 KG)
HEAVIEST KNOWN WOLF

1974
FIRST YEAR ON ENDANGERED SPECIES LIST

42
TEETH

7 to 13 YEARS
LIFE SPAN

25 to 40 miles
(40 TO 64 KM)
PER HOUR
RUNNING SPEED

30
MILES
(48 KM)
PER DAY
TOP DISTANCE
TRAVELED
IN A DAY

CHAPTER 4

Predators
and Other Threats

Gray wolves have few **predators**. Humans have been their main threat. Gray wolves once lived in most of North America. But people built on the land where they lived. Hunters killed them.

For a time, gray wolves were almost **extinct**. Laws protect wolves and their homes today. Their numbers are growing.

Gray Wolves
in the United States

year	1963	1965	1967	1969	1971	1973	1975	1977	19
	600	600	600	700	700	700	1,100	1,100	

4,000 — 3,000 — 2,000 — 1,000 —

1,250　1,250　1,300　1,500　1,650　1,650　1,650　2,600　3,200　3,600

81　1983　1985　1987　1989　1991　1993　1995　1997　1999　2001

An Important Role

Wolves play a key role in their **ecosystems**. They clear out sick animals from herds and leave the fit ones. When they hunt, they may not eat all their prey. This food feeds others, such as bears.

A food chain shows links between animals and plants. This food chain shows what gray wolves eat. It also shows that nothing eats them.

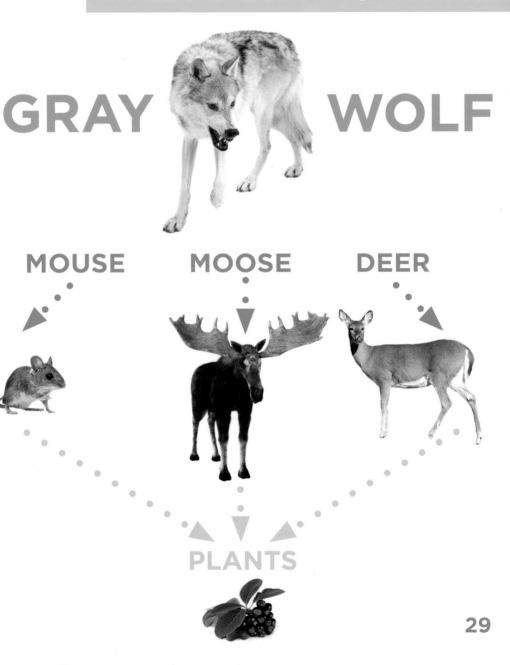

GRAY WOLF

MOUSE   MOOSE   DEER

PLANTS

GLOSSARY

carnivore (KAR-nuh-vor)—a meat-eating animal

ecosystem (E-co-sys-tum)—a community of living things in one place

extinct (ek-STINKT)—no longer existing

litter (LIH-tur)—the young born to an animal at a single time

pack (PAK)—a group of animals that hunts together

predator (PRED-uh-tuhr)—an animal that eats other animals

prey (PRAY)—an animal hunted or killed for food

range (RAYNJ)—the area where a certain animal naturally lives

tundra (TUN-druh)—a treeless land with a frozen layer below the surface

Books

Curtis, Jennifer Keats. *The Lucky Litter: Wolf Pups Rescued from Wildfire*. Mount Pleasant, SC: Arbordale Publishing, 2015.

Leaf, Christina. *Gray Wolves*. North American Animals. Minneapolis: Bellwether Media, Inc., 2015.

Marsh, Laura F. *Wolves*. National Geographic Readers. Washington, D.C.: National Geographic, 2012.

Websites

Gray Wolf
www.biokids.umich.edu/critters/Canis_lupus/

Gray Wolf
www.dkfindout.com/us/animals-and-nature/dogs/gray-wolf/

Wild Kids
www.wolf.org/learn/wild-kids/